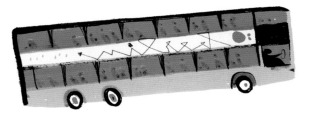

Capitals

Visit the World's
Capital Cities!

by Taraneh Ghajar Jerven
illustrated by Nik Neves and Nina de Camargo

Blueprint
EDITIONS

Contents

What is a Capital?	6	Mexico City	22
Washington, D.C.	8	New Delhi	24
Rome	10	Clean, Green cities	26
Tokyo	12	Beijing	28
London	14	Copenhagen	30
Architecture	16	Abu Dhabi	32
Nairobi	18	Canberra	34
Paris	20	Kuala Lumpur	36

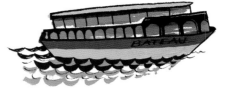

Warsaw	38	Bangkok	52
Buenos Aires	40	Moscow	54
Transportation	42	Reykjavík	56
Amsterdam	44	Berlin	58
Cairo	46	Capitals of the World	60
Havana	48	Find the Capital	62
Other Key Capitals	50	Credits	64

Red arrows scattered throughout the book indicate where sights do not fall on the map, as they may be some distance away from the city center.

What is a Capital?

The identity of any city is a combination of people, geography, customs, and historical events. Capital cities are where a country's government is located, making them unique, but they are also so much more than this. In many cases, the capital city is also the country's center for trade and culture. London, England; Paris, France; and Havana, Cuba, are all examples of capitals that grew around an important trading port on a river or ocean. They are now amazing hubs with fascinating museums, delicious food, and jaw-dropping art and architecture.

Cairo, Egypt, and Rome, Italy, are two ancient and incredible cities that have maintained power in their respective countries over many thousands of years. They have the mysterious ruins of buildings and monuments to prove it. Once in a while, a country even invents a capital city—for example, Australia designed Canberra to be the capital because its two largest cities, Sydney and Melbourne, kept fighting over which should have the title.

It's time to scout out the key landmarks and quirky daily life of some of the world's capital cities. What are they famous for? Where are the best places to visit? How do the people who live there eat, dress, and play? The beautiful maps are illustrated representations of the cities, giving you an incredible taste of some of the world's capitals, and showing the approximate locations of many amazing landmarks. Let's go discover!

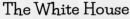

The White House
The first president of the United States, George Washington, selected the site for the White House in 1791. Every US president since John Adams has lived there. The White House has 132 rooms and 35 bathrooms over six floors.

Ford's Theater
Famously the site of President Abraham Lincoln's assassination, Ford's Theater is now a museum that offers talks, artifacts, and a reenactment of the assassination.

The Washington Monument
Built to commemorate George Washington, this 554-foot-tall obelisk on the National Mall is both the world's tallest obelisk and the world's largest stone structure.

The Lincoln Memorial
Built to commemorate the sixteenth President of the United States, the Lincoln Memorial contains a sculpture of Abraham Lincoln and inscriptions of two of his well-known speeches.

Native American History
Before Europeans discovered North America, there were lots of different tribes of people living on the land. Washington, D.C., is home to the National Museum of the American Indian.

Martin Luther King Jr. Memorial
Located in West Potomac Park, the memorial covers 4 acres and includes the *Stone of Hope*, a granite statue of civil rights leader Martin Luther King Jr.

Washington, D.C. (District of Columbia), USA, was founded on July 16, 1790, when James Madison, Thomas Jefferson, and Alexander Hamilton came to a compromise where they declared George Washington's selection of a site on the Potomac River to be the nation's capital in exchange for the government assuming the debts from the Revolutionary War.

Washington, D.C., has been the political and defense capital of the United States since then, housing the President of the United States, the United States Congress, and the Pentagon (right across the Potomac River).

The Smithsonian

Founded in 1846, the Smithsonian consists of 19 museums and galleries, the National Zoological Park, and nine research facilities. The collection includes the Ruby Slippers from the *Wizard of Oz*, the Apollo Command Module, and many amazing dinosaur skeletons.

The Capitol

The Capitol Building sits on Capitol Hill and is the home of the United States Congress.

Library of Congress

This research library claims to be the largest library in the world. It holds books in more than 450 languages.

United States Botanical Gardens

Established in 1820, the US Botanical Gardens are among the oldest in North America.

WASHINGTON, D.C.

The city of Rome, Italy, was founded in 753 BCE. According to legend, two brothers (and demigods), Romulus and Remus, were left for dead, saved by a river god, and then raised by a wolf. After putting the rightful king (and their grandfather) back on the throne, they set out to build a city of their own. Romulus killed Remus after a dispute over where to build the city, and he then named the city after himself.

Rome was the capital of the Papal States until 1870, then of the Kingdom of Italy in 1871. It then became the capital of the Italian Republic in 1946. It has a population of 4.3 million residents and is extremely famous for its ancient architecture and many, many religious artworks.

The Pope and Swiss Guard
The Pope is the Bishop of Rome and the worldwide leader of the Catholic Church. The Swiss Guard is a tiny army responsible for the safety of the Pope.

Passeggiata
Many Italians take part in this traditional leisurely stroll during the evening. This is usually done for the purpose of socializing in the central piazza, or park.

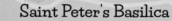

Saint Peter's Basilica

Vatican City State
Vatican City is a walled enclave within the city of Rome, and it is the smallest state in the world. To be a citizen of Vatican City, you have to work for the Holy See—the Catholic Church. It is ruled by the Bishop of Rome, the Pope.

Food
Rome is well-known for having lots of delicious foods, but their excellent gelato, pizza, and espresso (a very strong coffee!) are some of the most popular. *Buon appetito!*

Parks
Alongside its bustling tourist areas, Rome has some of the most beautiful parks in Europe. Originally gardens for luxury villas, Rome's many parks are free and open to the public.

ROMA

Fiumi Fountain

The Spanish Steps
Tourists come to Rome every year to visit the amazing historical sights, from the Fiumi Fountain to the Spanish Steps to perhaps the best preserved ancient Roman building, the Pantheon.

Trevi Fountain
This iconic fountain is a favorite of tourists visiting Rome and has been featured in many films. It is estimated that $3,565 (€3,000) are tossed into the fountain every day. The money is collected and given to a charity for the poor.

The Pantheon
Legend says this magnificent temple was built on the spot where Romulus ascended to heaven. It is the best-preserved ancient Roman monument, surviving time, fire, storms, and barbarian raids.

Colosseum
The most recognizable part of Roman history, the Colosseum was used for gladiatorial contests, chariot racing, and much more. It could seat 50,000 people and is the biggest ampitheater ever built.

Basilica of Santa Maria in Trastevere

Mouth of Truth
The Bocca della Verità is a marble mask that stands against the wall in the Church of Santa Maria in Cosmedin. It was possibly originally used as a drain cover!

東京

Shinjuku Gyoen National Garden
Considered the most beautiful garden in Tokyo, Shinjuku used to be just for the emperor. These days, he shares! The park has traditional Japanese gardens and pavilions, as well as English and French gardens.

Meiji shrine
This shrine was dedicated to Emperor Meiji and the Empress Shoken in 1920. Emperor Meiji (1852–1912) was the first emperor of modern Japan.

Tokyo Tower
From the top of this 1,092-foot steel tower, visitors can see all of Tokyo. Six hundred stairs or a ride in an elevator takes you to the top. If it looks like the Eiffel Tower, that was the plan!

Shibuya crossing and shopping area
This incredibly bright, busy, and colorful shopping area is where fashion trends are invented and locals come to eat and have fun. Anything can happen here under the flashing neon signs.

Tokyo National Museum
Established in 1872, TNM is the largest art museum in Japan and a must-see museum in Tokyo. The collection of 110,000 treasures includes ancient samurai swords and silk kimonos.

Ueno Park
In spring, Tokyo's most popular park is the place to enjoy cherry blossoms from the 1,000 trees lining the paths. Many museums are located here.

Senso-ji Temple
Tokyo's oldest Buddhist temple was completed in 645 CE. Visitors enter through the dramatic red *Kaminarimon* (Thunder Gate) to see a striking five-story pagoda. Outside, it is popular to shop for Japanese street food and souvenirs.

Imperial Palace
The emperor's home was completed in 1888. The palace sits in the city center on the former site of Edo Castle, surrounded by moats and stone walls.

Tokyo is home to the Japanese Emperor and the seat of the government, and it is also the financial capital of Japan. There are more people squeezed into this capital than any other city in the world, with more than 13 million people living in the center.

Tokyo has very special contrasts—peaceful traditional Japanese gardens oppose the busy urban crush. It has a fun devotion to pop culture, from kitties and robots to anime and manga books. It also boasts many Michelin-starred restaurants. Sushi, noodles, or an eight-course meal—people come here to eat!

Tsukiji Food Market
Tsukiji is the largest fish market in the world. Because it's so popular among Japanese and international visitors, it also serves excellent Japanese street snacks such as ramen and sweet buns alongside raw fish.

Kabukiza Theater
Kabuki is a type of Japanese theater where stories are acted out using song, mime, and dance. The place to experience it is the Kabukiza Theater, which was built in 1889.

London

Regent's Park
Regent's is possibly the most fun Royal Park. It has the London Zoo, where the bear who inspired Winnie the Pooh once lived. It also boasts a boating lake, sporting fields, an outdoor theater, and a rose garden.

Oxford Street/Regent Street shopping and theater district
The busiest shopping area in London is Oxford Street, with historic department stores such as Selfridges. Regent Street has fancier boutiques including Hamley's, one of London's oldest toy stores.

Hyde Park
Near Kensington Palace, this huge park has all the delights of childhood fun including a pirate playground, horseback riding, and a serpent-shaped boating and swimming lido. Keep an eye out for the park's green parakeets!

Buckingham Palace
Since 1837, Buckingham Palace has been home to the reigning king or queen. The palace has 775 rooms. Many famous guests have visited, including Gandhi, who wore a loincloth and sandals to tea with the king.

Victoria and Albert Museum
The V&A is the world's largest museum of decorative arts and design. Inside, you'll find 4.5 million jaw-dropping examples of fashion, sparkly jewelry, bizarre furniture, and delicate ceramics.

Westminster Abbey
Coronations and royal weddings take place at Westminster, a gothic architectural marvel built from the thirteenth to the sixteenth centuries. It also houses the graves of famous people such as writer Charles Dickens and Queen Elizabeth I.

St. Paul's Cathedral
This famous landmark was completed in 1710 by Sir Christopher Wren. There are 528 stairs to reach the top of the dome.

Tower of London
William the Conqueror built this fortress, palace, and prison on the Thames in 1066 to scare invaders. Today, the tower protects the Crown Jewels. Six ravens live here; legend says the kingdom will fall if they ever leave.

The London Eye
This eye-catching, super-sized Ferris wheel on the South Bank offers thrilling views of London to millions of visitors each year.

Tower Bridge
One of the most famous bridges in the world, Tower Bridge handles road and water traffic. It has two bascules that lift so that tall ships can sail upriver.

London became the capital of Great Britain in the twelfth century. The city has overcome Viking attacks, fires, plagues, and the blitz bombings of World War II, growing into one of the most powerful cities in the world.

London is the largest city in the UK and among the largest in Europe. The capital is famous for its diversity—over 300 languages are spoken here. Visitors love London for its green parks, amazing museums, and quirky British symbols including the Queen's guards in furry bearskin hats, red double-decker buses, and black cabs. Historic landmarks such as Big Ben and Tower Bridge sit next to modern icons like the London Eye. A bird's-eye view from the top of this observation wheel is a great way to see the contrasts.

Big Ben and Houses of Parliament
The Palace of Westminster is the meeting place for the House of Lords and the House of Commons. The highlight is the iconic clocktower with bell Big Ben, which weighs more than two fully grown elephants!

Architecture

Architecture is the art and science of designing your environment, including buildings. Buildings come in all shapes and sizes. Flower temples, sharp needles, round arenas, twin towers, and bent skyscrapers are all possible. Throughout history, buildings reflect location. People around the world use the building materials they have available, from bricks to wood to stone, building for their climate and geography. No matter how creative or crazy the idea, the building must stand. Architects design buildings to last.

Petronas Towers—Kuala Lumpur (1996)
The tallest twin towers in the world, at 1,483 feet, are shaped like an Islamic star if viewed from above.

The Shard—London (2012)
The Shard is home to London's highest viewing platform and stands at an impressive 1,000 feet.

Palace of Culture and Science—Warsaw (1955)
Standing at 778 feet from the base to the tip of the spire, the tallest building in Poland was a gift from Russia.

Brasília Cathedral—Brasília (1970)
This 131-foot unusual modernist cathedral looks like hands reaching to heaven.

Colosseum—Rome (80 CE)
Rome's arena for gladiatorial games is the largest amphitheater ever built. It measures 511 feet wide and 164 feet tall.

Parthenon—Athens (438 BCE)
This 45-foot white marble temple has stood tall on the hill of the Acropolis for more than 2,000 years.

The White House—Washington, D.C. (1800)
The US president's house was inspired by both the Irish Parliament building and Greek architecture. It is 150 feet wide and 68 feet tall.

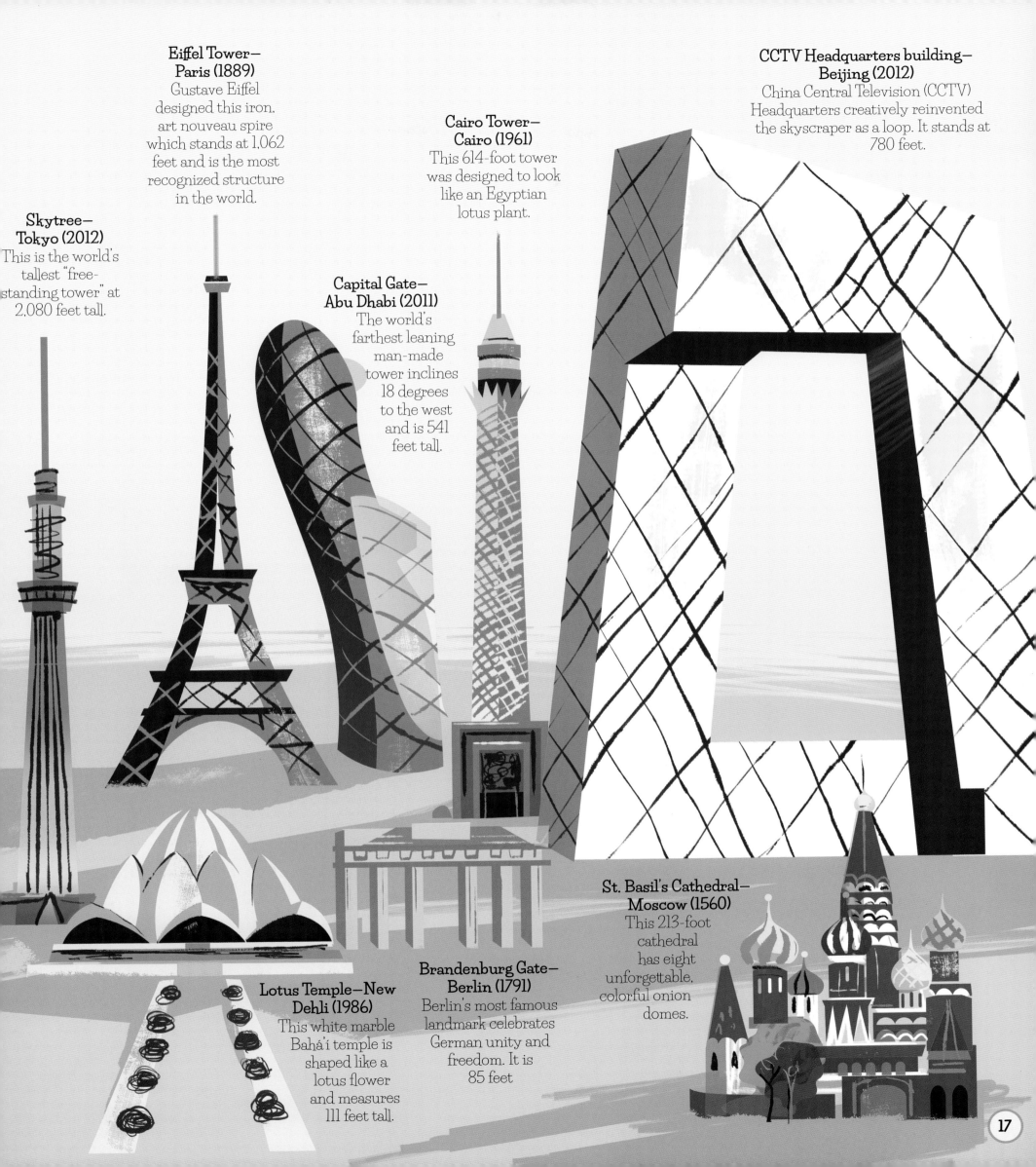

Skytree—Tokyo (2012)
This is the world's tallest "free-standing tower" at 2,080 feet tall.

Eiffel Tower—Paris (1889)
Gustave Eiffel designed this iron, art nouveau spire which stands at 1,062 feet and is the most recognized structure in the world.

Cairo Tower—Cairo (1961)
This 614-foot tower was designed to look like an Egyptian lotus plant.

Capital Gate—Abu Dhabi (2011)
The world's farthest leaning man-made tower inclines 18 degrees to the west and is 541 feet tall.

CCTV Headquarters building—Beijing (2012)
China Central Television (CCTV) Headquarters creatively reinvented the skyscraper as a loop. It stands at 780 feet.

Lotus Temple—New Dehli (1986)
This white marble Bahá'í temple is shaped like a lotus flower and measures 111 feet tall.

Brandenburg Gate—Berlin (1791)
Berlin's most famous landmark celebrates German unity and freedom. It is 85 feet

St. Basil's Cathedral—Moscow (1560)
This 213-foot cathedral has eight unforgettable, colorful onion domes.

NAIROBI

Ngong Forest Sanctuary

Leopards, bushbucks, hyenas, and baboons all live in this rare urban forest in the heart of Nairobi. Visitors flock here for walks, cycling, and even horseback riding.

Where else can you watch giraffes and zebras roam free with glittering skyscrapers in the background? Perched on Kenya's highlands with parkland right outside the city, Nairobi has earned the title "World Wildlife Capital" because it is so safari-friendly. Nairobi became the capital of Kenya in 1963 after the country won independence. It is a multicultural city with many different tribes represented. This city is packed with exciting cultural attractions. In addition to meeting wild animals in Nairobi National Park and the urban forests, you can also visit the Nairobi National Museum in this city.

Sigiria Karura Forest

An orange waterfall, secret Mau Mau caves, and pythons are just some of the amazing experiences in this dense forest.

David Sheldrick Wildlife Trust

Park warden David Sheldrick is famous for saving orphaned baby rhinos and elephants. Watch these little friends take a mud bath at the orphanage in Nairobi National Park.

Karen Blixen Museum

This bungalow at the foot of the Ngong hills belonged to author Karen Blixen from 1917 to 1931. She became famous for her stories.

Giraffe Center Nature Reserve

Visitors hand-feed and kiss endangered Rothschild's giraffes at this special habitat. They are bred here then released into the wild.

National Museum of Nairobi

Kenya's National Museum displays East African history alongside ancient skulls of early man and artifacts from the tribes of Kenya.

BAPS Shri Swaminarayan Mandir

This impressive Hindu temple was the first traditional stone and marble temple to be built in Africa.

Jamia Mosque

The biggest mosque in Nairobi and the most important in Kenya, Jamia stands out because of its three silver domes. It was built in 1906 for Syed Maulana Abdullah Shah.

Uhuru Park

This 32-acre park is in the core of the business district. Top sights include a man-made lake and the Kenya National Monument. It is very popular with skateboarders.

Nairobi Railway Museum

Check out vintage locomotives, follow a miniature train, and climb on a passenger coach at the Railway Museum—right next to Nairobi's railway station.

Nairobi National Park

The only safari park in the world that borders a capital city is home to black rhinos, giraffes, lions, leopards, baboons, zebras, wildebeests, and 400 bird species.

Arc de Triomphe
Napoléon commissioned the Arc in 1806 to celebrate his victories. It took 30 years to finish. One pilot has even flown a plane through it! Visitors climb 284 stairs for spectacular city views.

Champs-Élysées
Ritzy boutiques and grand cafés line one of the world's loveliest avenues.

L'Opéra de Paris

Dome of the Invalides

Eiffel Tower
People line up every day to climb this iconic tower, which was originally built as a temporary exhibit for the 1889 World's Fair. The lacy iron tower is 1,063 feet tall and weighs a whopping 10,100 tons!

Musée d'Orsay
The Orsay has a world-famous Impressionist painting collection with works by Van Gogh, Monet, and Courbet. The building is cool too; it's a former train station.

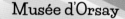

Paris

For centuries, Paris has been one of the world's most influential and dazzling cities. Nicknamed *La Ville Lumière* (City of Light), Paris is historically the source of big ideas as well as beauty. It is known for rebellion, culture, and cuisine.

Paris has been the capital of France on and off since 900 CE, most recently from 1944 to the present day. With more than 12 million inhabitants, Paris is home to almost 20 percent of the French population. The city is made up of the Left Bank, Right Bank, and central island areas on the Seine River. It is divided into 20 neighborhoods known as *arrondissements*.

Sacré-Cœur
Climb Montmartre, the biggest hill in Paris, and find this snow-white Catholic basilica, built from 1875–1914. There are 300 stairs to take you to the top.

Pompidou Center
Have you ever seen an inside-out building? Renzo Piano and Richard Rogers designed this marvelous modern art museum with mechanics such as escalators on the exterior. It is the largest modern art museum in Europe.

The Louvre
Nine million visitors a year explore the largest museum in the world, with 35,000 masterpieces and ancient treasures. Must-sees include Leonardo's *Mona Lisa* and the Venus de Milo sculpture.

Notre-Dame
The most visited monument in France is this enormous Gothic cathedral built from the twelfth to the fourteenth centuries. It has some amazing sculptures, including iconic gargoyles.

Sainte-Chapelle
With 15 stained glass windows, each standing 49 feet tall, this thirteenth-century church is astonishingly colorful on a sunny day.

The Panthéon
The Panthéon is a mausoleum—a fancy tomb—for famous French men and women including Alexandre Dumas, author of *The Three Musketeers.*

Jardin du Luxembourg
Toy sailboats, a puppet theater, and a carousel are some of the amusements for kids at this magnificent garden. Queen Marie de' Medici had them built in 1612 to remind her of her childhood.

CIUDAD de MÉXICO

National Museum of Anthropology
This popular museum displays exciting artifacts of pre-Hispanic Mexico, including massive Mayan and Aztec stone carvings of animals.

Wrestling
Lucha libre wrestling is a popular pastime in Mexico City, with colorfully masked wrestlers called luchadores fighting in a ring. There are elaborate heroes and villains and crowds cheer for their favorites.

National History Museum
Housed in the Castillo de Chapultepec— home of the Mexican president until 1939— this museum tells the story of Mexico from colonial days through to the revolution. Don't miss the sword used by José María Morelos in the War of Independence.

Chapultepec Park
This park is a key weapon in Mexico City's fight against pollution. Its 1,695 acres of plants replenish the city's fresh air. Chapultepec is one of the largest parks in the world and contains Aztec ruins, museums, and a zoo.

Papalote Museum (Children's Museum)
This indoor and outdoor museum is bursting with interactive exhibits on space, ecology, art, the human body, science, and music.

Parque Alameda Central

This park was founded in 1529 on the former Aztec marketplace. It sits next to the Palacio de Bellas Artes and is known for its fountains.

Museo Mural Diego Rivera

When an earthquake destroyed much of the hotel housing Diego Rivera's famous mural *Dream of a Sunday Afternoon in the Alameda Central*, the city opened a museum to protect the painting. The mural depicts famous historical figures from the city's history.

Templo Mayor and the Great Pyramid of Tenochtitlan

In 1978, workers accidentally discovered the long lost Templo Mayor, which sits atop a mighty pyramid on the exact spot where the Aztecs founded Mexico City.

Palace of Fine Arts

Top notch performers, such as the Ballet Folklórico de México, take the stage at this magnificent white and gold palace. The building is famous for its fancy interior and murals by great Mexican painters.

National Palace

Aztec emperor Moctezuma II built the first palace on this spot. In 1521, the fierce Spanish conquistador Hernán Cortés seized and rebuilt it. Today, the grand building houses the offices of the president of Mexico. The twentieth-century Diego Rivera murals inside tell the story of Mexican civilization.

Sitting in the Valley of Mexico, convenient for trade routes crossing the country, Mexico City is the oldest continuously inhabited city in the Western Hemisphere. A staggering 21 million people live in the greater metropolitan area, making it one of the most populated cities in the West.

Due to overcrowding, Mexico City struggles with pollution. It is both a gorgeous and a gritty city. A walk can reveal ancient ruins, colonial buildings, and slick modern architecture. The city's culinary scene is now globally recognized.

Gurudwara Bangla Sahib

Snow-white marble and golden onion domes make this Sikh temple a showstopper. Many believe the *sarovar* (pool) inside has healing powers. They serve daily *langar* (free meals) to the needy.

Jama Masjid

India's largest mosque was completed in 1658 and can fit 25,000 people inside. It took 5,000 workers and cost a million rupees to build—a huge sum in those days!

This mega metropolis has been an ancient capital of India on and off since the sixth century BCE. It is situated on the Yamuna River, which is sacred in Hinduism.

The city is divided into Old Delhi and New Delhi. Visiting Old Delhi feels like traveling back in time. The narrow alleys are stuffed with small shops selling everything from spices to gold and tea. Street food peddlers, bicycles, and rickshaws clog the streets. In contrast, New Delhi is spacious, with grand colonial buildings such as the president's palace, laid out on a green grid.

India Gate

This 138-foot-tall stone memorial arch honors the 90,000 Indian army soldiers who died in the first World War, the Northwest Frontier operations, and the Anglo-Afghan War.

National Museum

Over 200,000 dazzling treasures from Indian civilization are stored here, some up to 5,000 years old. They include musical instruments, jewelry, weapons, Buddhist relics, and art.

National Rail Museum

Railways are the most important form of transportation in India. If you think riding a train means roughing it, peek at the Maharaja's royal saloon train car. Catch a ride on the mini train that circles the museum grounds.

Gandhi Smriti and Gandhi memorial

Gandhi (1869–1948), the famous activist who taught the world how to protest peacefully, lived the last part of his life in Birla House, where the memorial stands.

Chandni Chowk

Chandni Chowk is one of the oldest, busiest markets in India. You can find almost anything in the colorful stalls. For a sweet treat, try a *jalebi*—a deep-fried sugar pretzel.

The Red Fort

Shah Jahan, the fifth Mughal Emperor of India, built this intricate red sandstone fort and palace, completed in 1638. The octagon-shaped complex has turrets, bastions, and other impressive flourishes.

उर्दू

नई दिल्ली

National Handicrafts and Handlooms Museum

India is known for its crafts; from vibrant embroidered cloth, to fancy gold work, to wood carvings. See beautiful crafts here, and shop for them too in the shady courtyard. Don't miss the wooden chariot!

Akshardham

This stunning Hindu spiritual center was built using ancient techniques to carve the pink sandstone. Don't miss the Sahaj Anand water show, where fountains shoot dancing jets of water.

National Zoological Park

This zoo is so large that visitors can choose to zip around on battery-operated vehicles. The most thrilling animals that live here include pythons, cobras, Himalayan bears, and royal white Bengal tigers.

Clean, Green Cities

When we talk about green cities, we are talking about cities that are sustainable. Living sustainably means avoiding using up Earth's natural resources and taking care of where you live so that it is possible for future generations to live there.

More than half the people in the world live in cities, and most of the world's energy is used up in cities. In crowded cities there is more waste, more smog from traffic fumes, and also more garbage. It is very important to fix the way we live in cities if we want to keep our planet safe.

Renewable Energy Sources—Tokyo

Earth will eventually run out of fossil fuel energy resources like oil, but energy from the sun and wind is renewable. Tokyo has floating solar panel farms to capture the sun's heat. Many cities are partially powered by wind farms in the countryside or out at sea.

Bicycles and Bike Lanes—Amsterdam/Copenhagen

Cities such as Amsterdam and Copenhagen have built many bike paths so that citizens can zip around on bicycles, which don't pollute the air like cars.

Solar-powered "Trees" — Singapore
Singapore has created a mechanical forest of man-made trees that can generate solar power.

Parks and Green Spaces — Stockholm
Cities have parks because people need to play and exercise. Parks also clean and cool the air, and they are beautiful. One third of Stockholm is made up of parks, including the entire island of Djurgården.

City Greenbelt — Ottawa
Cities often swallow the forests and farms around them. To prevent this, Ottawa made a greenbelt around the city protecting 49,421 acres of land including farms, forests, and wetlands.

Great Public Transport — Helsinki
Cars that run on gasoline or diesel make exhaust fumes that are harmful to the planet. Helsinki has excellent bus, tram, and metro connections so people don't need to use cars as much.

Control of Vehicle Emissions — Berlin
Since car pollution is so bad for human health, Berlin has created zones where only environmentally-friendly cars can drive.

Recycling and Waste Management — Vienna
We can avoid waste by reusing things, recycling materials like plastic and paper, and turning kitchen scraps into compost. Vienna is the best city in Europe for recycling and waste treatment.

27

Beijing Zoo

At this special zoo, the grounds are designed like Chinese classical gardens, and the staff breed rare Chinese animals including pandas, tigers, and giant salamanders.

The Great Wall of China (Badaling section)

China's most impressive engineering feat is a stone wall that stretches 13,170 miles east to west along its entire border. The Badaling section stands at 26 feet tall and 20 feet wide, and five horses can gallop abreast on top!

北京

Beijing has been the political and cultural heart of China for nearly eight centuries. With 21.5 million residents, it has more people than any capital in the world. It is also one of the largest cities worldwide.

Mysterious ancient palaces such as the Forbidden City, *hútòng* (tiny alleys), red and gold temples, and the Great Wall of China sit alongside jaw-dropping feats of newfangled architecture. Beijing modernized so quickly that it seems like its skyline is constantly changing. You'll find first-class museums and galleries here. Beijing is also great for eating out—you can taste snacks from every corner of China.

Beijing Temple of Confucius
Built in 1302, this temple honors the Chinese philosopher Confucius who taught ethics. He believed in *ren*, or loving others.

Lama Temple
This red and gold Tibetan Buddhist temple is known for a 59-foot Buddha *Maitreya* (Buddha of the Future) statue carved from sandalwood.

Beihai Park
The oldest and largest ancient imperial garden in China features a beautifully painted Nine-Dragon screen wall and a lake where the fierce Kublai Khan had an island palace.

Jingshan Park
This lovely urban park has a hill made from the dirt that was dug up to build the moat around the Forbidden City.

Forbidden City
If you entered the Forbidden City without permission during the reign of the emperors, the penalty was death. The ancient palace was built by the best Chinese craftsmen, and it has a moat and a wall.

Imperial Palace Museum
This enormous palace is stuffed with priceless treasures, from jade and silks to gold thrones decorated with dragons.

National Museum of China
Head to Tiananmen Square to visit this large museum. Over a million fascinating artifacts tell the story of China, from man's ancestors 1.7 million years ago through to the modern day.

Meridian Gate
This gate runs through the heart of Beijing, and it was once believed to be the heart of the universe.

Tiananmen Square
The world's largest public square is named after the Tiananmen Gate that separates it from the Imperial City.

Temple of Heaven
More a park than a temple, this peaceful Confucian complex was built in 1420 for the emperor to pray for a good harvest. In 1918, the space became a public park.

KØBENHAVN

Botanical Gardens
Nestled in the heart of Copenhagen, the Botanical Gardens are impossible to miss. Glass greenhouses contain over 13,000 species of plants.

Rundetaarn
The oldest working observatory in Europe was built in 1642. Instead of stairs, it has a spectacular spiral pathway.

Rosenborg Castle
This fairy-tale 400-year-old renaissance castle has gorgeous gardens. The Knights' Hall has royal thrones and three life-sized silver lions standing guard. The Danes also keep the crown jewels here.

Christiansborg Palace
One of six palaces and castles in Copenhagen, Christiansborg is important because it houses the Danish Parliament and the supreme court. The queen also houses 20 white horses and a golden carriage here.

Frederiksberg Gardens
This rambling park was once the gardens of King Frederik IV's summer palace. Today it's a great spot for picnics and boating. The Copenhagen Zoo is next door; you can peek at the elephants from the park!

Tivoli Gardens
Hair-raising rides, magical gardens, and memorable shows characterize the amusement park Tivoli, which has been entertaining and inspiring visitors since 1843. Christmas at Tivoli is especially festive.

National Museum of Denmark
Located in the Prince's Palace, the museum's highlights include Viking ships, a 2,000-year-old mummy, and a dress-up wardrobe with old-fashioned costumes.

Kastellet

This star-shaped fortress with a moat has been keeping watch over Copenhagen since the 1600s.

The Little Mermaid

Copenhagen's national symbol is the sculpture of the little mermaid from the fairy tale by author Hans Christian Andersen. The life-sized bronze girl is perched on a granite rock in the harbor.

Amalienborg Palaces

Amalienborg is the royal residence. Don't miss the changing of the royal guard at noon, performed with a lively marching band.

Nyhavn

The historic canal port is lined with multicolored townhouses. Three hundred years ago, sailors came to Nyhavn to party. Today, it's the place to eat seafood and embark on a boat ride.

Copenhagen has been the political and commercial capital of Denmark since 1443. The royal family and the parliament are located there. The city has survived plague and fire in the eighteenth century and the German occupation during the Second World War.

Today, it is famous for a cool mix of creative modern architecture and colorful historic architecture. Residents bike everywhere. The magical amusement park Tivoli has been making people happy for over 100 years. It's not surprising that Copenhagen is always on top ten lists of the world's most pleasant cities.

Emirates Park Zoo
Imagine feeding hungry Indian elephants, a Nile crocodile, or climbing a ladder to reach a hungry giraffe. There are 1,700 animals to see at the zoo, including a pair of white tigers.

Saadiyat Island
Of all of Abu Dhabi's islands, Saadiyat has the most amazing beach. The white sand and turquoise waters are pretty, but the real draw is the endangered Hawksbill sea turtles.

Marina Eye
Marina Mall is a modern day souk (Arab bazaar) where locals come to escape the heat, shop, and hang out. It is famous for its Ferris wheel, giving shoppers a bird's-eye view of the city.

Qasr al-Hosn Fort
This coral and sea stone watchtower was built in the 1760s. The sheikhs of the Bani Yas tribe used it to protect trade routes. The coral and shell fort walls sparkled in the sun, providing a lighthouse for the merchant boats.

Observation Deck at 300
Built in 2006, the glass Etihad Towers soar over Abu Dhabi, symbolizing the city's modern and luxurious identity. On the 74th floor, brave visitors can have high tea 984 feet in the air while taking in a view of the city and islands.

The United Arab Emirates is made up of seven desert kingdoms, and the largest one is Abu Dhabi. It became the capital in the 1990s.

About 1.5 million people live in this sweltering hot beach city. Abu Dhabi's skyline is very modern and made up of glittering skyscrapers against the turquoise Persian Gulf. The city grew very wealthy, first from pearl diving, and later from oil revenue. Even though it is a supermodern city, residents still enjoy traditional pastimes such as shopping in *souks* (markets), training falcons, and camel racing.

أبوظبي

Abu Dhabi Beaches
Abu Dhabi has over 250 miles of coastline, though only 6 miles of this is open to the public. The rest is made up of private beaches.

Yas Waterworld
Visitors beat the Abu Dhabi heat at this futuristic waterpark on Yas Island. It is home to 45 wet rides, a tornado waterslide with a 65-foot-tall funnel, and wave pools.

Emirates Heritage Village
Time travel back to life in an oasis desert village before the UAE grew rich from the discovery of oil. Visitors can peek inside a Bedouin goat's hair tent, shop for spices at the souk, and meet a camel.

Sheikh Zayed Grand Mosque
This enormous white and gold mosque is always at the top of the list of must-see global landmarks. It has 82 marble domes and over 1,000 pillars, doubled by long reflecting pools. More than 40,000 people can pray here at one time on the world's largest handloomed carpet.

Ferrari World
The extreme wow-factor at this car-themed amusement park is 100 percent modern Abu Dhabi. It took more steel than three Eiffel Towers to build and more space than seven football fields! Among all the rides, the draw is Formula Rossa—the fastest rollercoaster in the world.

Abu Dhabi Falcon Hospital
Bedouins have used falcons for hunting in the desert for centuries. These days, they are treasured pets. At this hospital, the noble birds are allowed to fly free. If you're brave, they'll perch on your arm for a photo.

CANBERRA

Australian National Botanic Gardens
Visitors can scout out the Australian bushland on the Discovery Trail. Be prepared to encounter swallowtail butterflies, water dragons, bats, bees, and even kangaroos.

Black Mountain Nature Park
Just behind the Botanic Gardens sits Black Mountain—the most diverse of Canberra's nature parks. Find 100 species of bird, 500 species of plant, and 5,000 species of insect. You might surprise reptiles sunning themselves on the path!

National Museum of Australia
Exhibits tell the stories of Australians, from the Aboriginals who lived here first to the British colonial era and the present day. Kspace, the interactive kids' adventure game, lets kids use a time pod to blast them back to Australia's past.

Lake Burley Griffin
Named after the man who designed Canberra, this man-made lake is at the heart of the capital. It is surrounded by a path that runs past the major museums and parks. Look out for the kangaroos by the Jerrabomberra Wetlands area.

National Zoo and Aquarium
Australia's national zoo specializes in close animal encounters. Visitors have the chance to feed white lions, sharks, giraffes, and more. Other must-see Australian animals that live here include pythons, koalas, dingoes, emus, and tree kangaroos.

Mount Ainslie Lookout
A pretty 2½ mile hike takes visitors from the War Memorial to the top of Mount Ainslie for spectacular views of the city. The path goes through Mount Ainslie Nature reserve.

Australian War Memorial
This impressive memorial honors Australian soldiers and includes a large commemorative area, a courtyard with a memorial pool, and a sculpture garden.

Commonwealth Park
This 86-acre park on the edge of Lake Burley Griffin is a popular spot for barbecues and concerts. Every year it hosts Floriade, Australia's largest spring festival, with a flower display grown from one million flower bulbs!

Aspen Island and National Carillon
Cross the footbridge from Kings Park to tiny Aspen Island to visit the National Carillon. The British government gave the 160-foot-tall structure to Canberra on the city's 50th anniversary as a capital. Picnic-friendly concerts are common here.

Questacon—The National Science and Technology Center
Over 200 interactive science exhibits offer amazing opportunities for discovery. Meet a robot, use video microscopes, and experience the strength of an earthquake.

National Gallery of Australia
The most famous work in this international collection is Jackson Pollock's splatter painted *Blue Poles*. Kids love to play in the mist from the outdoor *Fog Sculpture* by Fujiko Nakaya.

Old Parliament House
Home to the Museum of Australian Democracy, Old Parliament House was the seat of the Australian Parliament from 1927–88. The children's exhibition area, Play Up, explores human rights themes through play.

Few capital cities are as young and as carefully planned as Canberra. When Australia's biggest cities, Sydney and Melbourne, were fighting over which one would be the capital, they compromised and gave the title to Canberra in 1909. A competition was then held for the best city design. The winner, American architect Walter Burley Griffin, created a beautiful city with wide boulevards and green spaces on a man-made lake.

The Australian federal parliament is in Canberra, as is the office of the governor-general. Other highlights include the national museums and libraries.

Kualan Lumpur

Food markets
Wet markets, selling fresh meat, fish, and vegetables, open early in the morning before the sun is up. If you're not an early bird, many markets are buzzing until late in the day.

Sultan Abdul Samad Building
Built in 1897, this spectacular Mughal-style building has fancy brickwork, copper domes, and a 135-foot-tall clock tower.

Sri Mahamariamman Temple
KL's oldest Hindu temple was founded in 1873 and has an astonishing five-tiered tower. Try to count all 228 colorful idols as you gaze up the pyramid.

Kuala Lumpur Bird Park
At this aviary in tropical paradise, birds such as rainbow lorikeets and bright blue Indian peacocks fly free.

Kuala Lumpur Butterfly Park
Malaysia's national butterfly, the bird-sized birdwing, and over a hundred other gorgeous species live at this amazing butterfly habitat.

National Mosque of Malaysia
This star-shaped mosque, built in 1965 for Malay Muslims, has a blue-tiled umbrella roof and a 243-foot-tall minaret that calls people to pray.

Thean Hou Temple
Dragons and phoenixes fly from the six roofs of this breathtaking temple dedicated to the sea goddess Tian Hou.

Petronas Towers
The tallest twin towers in the world have a design inspired by Islamic architecture. Visitors ride up 41 floors and cross a stunning skybridge between the towers before making the final ascent.

Aquaria KLCC
Electric eels, rays, bright coral fish, piranhas, and 150 other salt- and freshwater species live in this immense oceanarium. Don't miss the tiger sharks in the underwater tunnel.

Menara Kuala Lumpur
With fantastic views of the city, this telecommunications tower also boasts a mini zoo and an upside-down house in the heart of a tropical rainforest.

K L, as most people call it, is named after the meeting place of the two rivers Gombak and Klang. Lumpur means muddy. In local slang, residents are called KLites, and 1.76 million KLites live in KL.

Kuala Lumpur, Malaysia, is an exciting hub because it's a cultural melting pot, mostly made up of Malays, Chinese, and Indians. You can visit food stalls and hawkers at fun street markets in Chinatown and Little India. The urban skyline is a cool mix of sparkling skyscrapers, including the world's tallest twin towers, next to mosque minarets. You'll even see old-fashioned Malay wood houses built on stilts. The climate is hot and rainy—this is tropical rainforest territory!

Istana Negara
This golden-domed palace was completed in 2011 and is the official residence of the Yang di-Pertuan Agong, the monarch of Malaysia.

WARSZAWA

Warsaw Barbican
These defense towers were built in 1540 to fortify Warsaw's walls. These days it's a good spot to find busker entertainment and pop-up art displays.

arsaw, Poland, is sometimes known as the Phoenix City because it has been destroyed by war many times and risen from the ashes. During the Second World War, much of the historic Old Town was reduced to rubble. When the city was rebuilt, its beauty and authenticity earned it UNESCO status. Today it is a striking mix of historic buildings and skyscrapers.

Historical Museum of Warsaw
This museum displays more than 7,000 objects of Warsaw by theme. A favorite is the room of Warsaw mermaids—the city symbol.

Old Town Market Square
This quaint square, lined with pastel townhouses, is in the center of the Old Town. It was originally used for the town hall, fairs, and executions.

Museum of Archaeology
This collection holds items ranging from an ancient Ice Age hut to golden treasure from early Polish rulers.

Sigismund's Column
One of Warsaw's most loved monuments, this 72-foot-tall column was erected in 1644 to honor King Sigismund.

Museum of Caricature and Cartoon Art
The world's only museum dedicated to comic drawings, this collection covers 20,000 works by Polish and foreign artists.

Lazienki Park
King Stanisław made Lazienki his summer home in 1764. Today, Lazienki is the largest park in Warsaw. It has many gorgeous gardens including a Chinese garden and a Royal Promenade with peacocks. Residents also enjoy the Royal Picture Gallery in his palace.

National Museum
Founded in 1862, this museum possesses a whopping 830,000 pieces of global and Polish art, ranging from ancient times to the present day.

Royal Castle

This brick castle was completely rebuilt after the Second World War, but the first building on the site dates back to the Middle Ages. Polish kings and queens have lived here since the sixteenth century, and the Polish president lived here until 1993. The triangular Castle Square in front is the entryway to the colorful Old Town.

City Zoological Garden

Today more than 5,000 animals reside at the Warsaw Zoo, from elephants and anteaters to sharks. At the hippo enclosure, visitors can watch the beasts swim underwater through

Presidential Palace

The home of the Polish president is a popular landmark to visit. Major events have taken place here, from Frederic Chopin's first performance at age 8 in 1818 to the signing of the Polish constitution in 1997.

Copernicus Science Center

Follow the lead of Copernicus, the famous mathematician and astronomer, and discover the natural world through observing and experimenting. The center also has a robot theater!

Colón Theater
Teatro Colón is one of the most important opera houses in the world. The acoustics are so good that the opera singers don't need to wear microphones! Completed in 1908, the fancy interior flaunts how rich Buenos Aires was at that time.

El Obelisco and Ave 9 de Julio
This 220-foot-tall needle monument was erected in 1936 to celebrate the 400th anniversary of the first Spanish settlement. It stands tall on Ave 9 de Julio, the widest avenue in the world with 16 lanes.

Bernardino Rivadavia Natural Sciences Museum
Visitors can explore Argentine biodiversity here. Don't miss the Sounds of Nature hall or the dinosaur bones dug up in Patagonia. The aquarium houses unusual freshwater fish, sea anemones, and tropical coral.

Subway
Subte, Buenos Aires's metro, is the oldest subway system in South America. It has been running for over 100 years, and it is used by over a million people every day!

Congress of Argentina
Modeled on the Capitol Building in Washington, D.C., the national congress building contains the two houses of the Argentine legislature—the senate and the chamber of deputies.

Plaza de Mayo
The square is named after the Argentine Revolution, which began in May 1810. It's the oldest city square in Buenos Aires, lined with landmarks including Casa Rosada.

K nown as the Paris of South America, Buenos Aires in Argentina is famous for its beauty and passion. A wave of Europeans from Spain and Italy immigrated to BA in the early twentieth century. The architecture therefore combines grand European style with colorful Latin American influences.

Buenos Aires has a reputation for nightlife. Restaurants serve dinner after 9 p.m.—they specialize in steak because of their huge cattle industry. Residents invented the world-famous tango dance late one night in the 1880s. It is normal to see residents dancing in the streets!

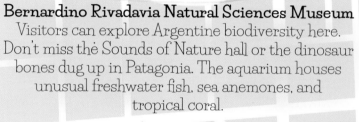

Centro Cultural Kirchner

In 2005, Néstor Kirchner had the ingenious idea to turn the huge 8-story post office building into a cultural center. It has a world-class concert hall and holds fun classes such as dance and yoga.

Casa Rosada, the Presidential Palace

Casa Rosada is the seat of the Argentine national government and the president's offices. It is thought to be pink because of the practice of mixing cow's blood with white paint to keep it from peeling.

Park Colon

The park in front of Casa Rosada is famous for the 20-foot-tall statue of Christopher Columbus, the Genoese explorer who sailed to Latin America in the fifteenth century. It honors 100 years of Argentine independence.

National Historical Museum

Created in 1880 to unify the divided Argentina after 50 years of civil war, the exhibits cover the revolution of 1810 and the Argentine War of Independence. The must-see artifact is the saber of hero José de San Martín.

Reserva Ecológica

Buenos Aires has 250 green spaces, and the Reserva is the largest at 865 acres. It sits on the east side of Puerto Madero, close to the city center. More than 300 bird species live here, so bring binoculars!

Transportation

There are many ways to get around in capital cities. Most cities have cars and taxis for hire, but often public transportation is faster, cheaper, and better for the environment. Many capitals, such as Mexico City, try to stop residents from driving cars to reduce traffic and smog. Public transportation can be anything from a double-decker London bus to a train, underground subway, or ferry boat. City dwellers also use small vehicles like bikes, mopeds, and rickshaws to get from here to there. These are handy in cities such as New Delhi, Rome, and Amsterdam, where many streets are ancient and narrow.

Train—Nairobi
Nairobi began as a railway depot, and trains are still incredibly important for connecting the region. In 2017, Kenya opened a major railway from Nairobi to Mombasa, the biggest infrastructure project since the country gained independence.

Boat—Paris
In Paris, you can explore the city's top landmarks from a batobus or *bateaux vedettes* (river boat) tour on the Seine that passes the Eiffel Tower, the Louvre, and Notre-Dame.

Black taxi—London
The black taxi or Hackney carriage is as much a symbol of London as Big Ben. They are going green (electric) from 2018 on, as the capital cleans up its dirty air.

Red bus—London
In 1907, when London bus companies competed for passengers, one bus company painted its buses red to stand out. Of course, they won!

Coco taxi—Havana
Coco taxis are small, three-wheeled motorized rickshaws used for transport in Cuba. They are round like coconuts, hence the cute name.

Ferry—Amsterdam
Amsterdam is a canal city with 1,200 bridges, but there are no bridges across Amsterdam's IJ River. Pedestrians, cyclists, and moped riders can catch a free ride on small city ferries.

Horse-drawn carriage—Vienna
Fiakers are horse-drawn carriages that were popular in Vienna until 1900.

Moped—Rome
Toylike *motorini* (motorized scooters) have been incredibly popular in Rome since the 1940s. The most iconic is the Vespa.

Bicycle—Copenhagen
From kids to kings, the Danish people cycle in any weather and any outfit. There are over 250 miles of bike lanes in Copenhagen and more bikes than inhabitants.

AMSTERDAM

Anne Frank Museum
See inside the secret apartment where a Jewish girl, Anne, and her family hid from the Nazis during WWII. It was here that she penned her famous diary about life under Nazi occupation.

Royal Palace
Amsterdam is so marshy that this palace needs 13,569 wooden stilts to stay propped up! Now used for royal functions, it was built to be the city hall during the Dutch Golden Age in the seventeenth century.

Rembrandt House
Take a peek at the studio where world-famous painter Rembrandt Harmenszoon van Rijn painted many of his masterpieces.

The port city of Amsterdam sits on the North Sea and the man-made lake IJmeer. The city, like the rest of the Netherlands, is flat. It is always in danger of flooding, as it is built on canals. There are 165 canals with 1,281 bridges. It takes 11 million wooden poles to keep Amsterdam's buildings from sinking into the mud. The city is also known for its love of bicycles, cool cafés, tulips, and art.

Amsterdam became the capital of the Netherlands in 1814, and it is the commercial center of the country. Oddly, the Dutch king and government are in The Hague.

Leidseplein
This buzzing square is the heart of the city. It's a great place to sample traditional Dutch food.

Vondelpark
Amsterdam's most popular park is enormous at 116 acres. With English gardens, winding paths, roller skate rentals, playgrounds, and a theater, it's no wonder everyone adores it!

Van Gogh Museum
Discover the largest collection of works by the great Dutch Post-Impressionist painter Vincent van Gogh (1853–1890) here. Don't miss the special *Sunflowers* painting.

NEMO Science Museum
This waterfront museum looks like a factory and has many interactive and fun displays. You can hear, touch, smell, and see how science works.

KNSM island
This once rundown dockland now has funky buildings, fancy shops, and bizarre bridges. The island is named after the Royal Dutch Steam Company (KNSM) because migrants used to set sail from here to America.

Hortus Botanicus
In the 1600s, Dutch doctors used this garden to make medicine. The oasis of 6,000 plants includes a 154-year-old lily and an agave cactus from the Roman era!

Natura Artis Magistra
This elegant nineteenth-century zoo is among the oldest in Europe. Over 900 animal species live in habitats ranging from the savannah to coral reefs. There's also a butterfly pavilion, insectarium, and planetarium.

Tropenmuseum
Inside a phenomenal brick building on the edge of the Oosterpark, visitors learn about other cultures, and it has famously fun adventures for kids.

القاهرة

Egyptian Museum
The Egyptian Museum owns one of the most awesome collections of ancient artifacts in the world. The highlights are the golden, bejeweled treasures of boy pharaoh Tutankhamun—King Tut—especially his solid gold funerary mask encrusted with semiprecious stones.

Egyptians call Cairo *Umm ad-Dunya*—"the mother of the world." For over 1,000 years, the ancient city has stood on the Nile River in a fertile green valley surrounded by desert.

Modern Cairo is a swarming and sprawling metropolis with an urban population of 12 million. It is the largest city in Africa. Cairo faces serious challenges with pollution, as the city lacks an efficient trash collection system and a public transportation network. Smog levels here can be alarming. On the other hand, access to ancient Egyptian treasures such as the pyramids of Giza and the Sphinx make it a thrilling place to explore.

Pyramids of Giza
The enormous tombs of the pharaohs are the last remaining wonders of the ancient world. The Great Pyramid has 2.3 million stones weighing an average of 2.5-15 tons each. It is so incredible that this was built 4,500 years ago. Thousands of slaves and farmers built the pyramids.

Sphinx monument
This enormous beast was carved around 2500 BCE and sports a lion's body and a human head. In Arabic, he is *Abu al-Hol* (Father of Terror). Nobody is quite sure who knocked off his nose!

Khan el-Khalili (bazaar)

Visitors and locals enjoy shopping in the bustling, narrow alleys of the fourteenth-century souk in search of spices and traditional trinkets made from gold and copper.

Al-Azhar Mosque

Cairo's oldest mosque was built in 970 CE and has been enlarged many times since. It has been a school since 988 CE, making it the second oldest learning institution in the world.

Abdeen Palace Museum

The Egyptian president often works from Abdeen Palace, built in 1874. The palace is one of the most fancily decorated palaces in the world. The on-site museum shows off official gifts, weapons, and documents.

Museum of Islamic Art

A Qur'an written in silver ink, handwoven carpets, and other artifacts are displayed at one of the world's most important collections of Muslim art.

Al-Azhar Park

This lovely park was created as part of a regeneration project. It commands spectacular views over the city.

Bab Zuweila

These mighty gates from Cairo's old city wall were built in 1092. The tall minarets functioned as lookouts for scouts. People believed one of the doors had healing powers.

The Citadel

Built in 1176 as a fort against crusaders, this large limestone building was home to the rulers of Egypt for 700 years. It's the perfect spot to glimpse the pyramids of Giza.

Mosque and Madrasa of Sultan Hassan

This mosque was built for Sultan Hassan between 1356 and 1363. Unfortunately, the sultan was assassinated before it was finished. It's famous for its large, peaceful courtyard.

Muhammad Ali Mosque

This white alabaster Turkish-style mosque, built between 1830 and 1848, is the most eye-catching in Cairo. The inside is decorated with sparkling chandeliers.

47

La HABANA

Museo Napoleónico

The theme at this quirky spot is Napoleon Bonaparte. Cuban sugar baron Julio Lobo collected over 7,000 objects associated with his life, from rare paintings to military equipment. It even has his bronze death mask.

Food

You can sample all sorts of tasty street food, like fresh fruit, mini pastries, doughnuts, and even delicious fruit shakes called *batido de mamey*.

Cars

For 40 years, it was against the law to buy a foreign car in Cuba, so Havana is full of amazing, old-fashioned cars straight out of the 1950s.

Revolution Square

Castro stood in this massive civic square to address his citizens. It's famous for a memorial to independence hero José Martí, as well as enormous murals of revolutionaries such as Che Guevara.

In 1607, Havana became the capital of Cuba. The city grew rich as the top Spanish colonial port traded sugar and slaves. Habaneros showed off by building a city of colorful architecture.

After the Cuban Revolution in 1959, when President Fidel Castro came to power, the city froze in time. Cars and buildings stayed old-fashioned and even started to crumble. Today, visitors are drawn to the city for its laid-back, retro vibes. As Cuba opens up to the world, it's unclear how long the capital will stay in a time warp.

Paseo del Prado
This old-world boulevard is an exciting strip for a lively stroll. Expect street soccer, salsa dancing, and pop-up markets. It connects old Havana and central Havana. Don't miss the two bronze lions, built in 1926.

Museum of the Revolution
The old Presidential Palace was transformed into a museum that tells the story of the Cuban Revolution, when socialist rebels overthrew dictator Fulgencio Batista in 1959. On the staircase, you can still see the bullet holes from when students attempted to execute him.

Havana Cathedral
Completed in 1789 for Havana's patron, San Cristóbal, this baroque cathedral is among the oldest in the Americas. It's built from cut coral, and you can spot marine fossils in the foundations.

Gran Teatro de la Habana
Built in 1915, this marble wedding cake of a theater on the Paseo del Prado is the headquarters of the Ballet Nacional de Cuba.

National Museum of the Fine Arts
The architecture here is as impressive as the collection, which is split into Cuban art and Universal art. Standout Cuban artists include Guillermo Collazo, the first great Cuban painter, and Rafael Blanco, known for cartoon drawings.

El Capitolio
Havana's grandest building, the National Capital Building, was built with 17 million pesos of sugar trade earnings in 1926. The 300-foot-tall dome is modeled on the Panthéon in Paris.

Plaza Veija (Old Square)
Funnily, when it was built in 1559, it was called *Plaza Nueva* (New Square). Lined with painted colonial and art nouveau architecture, the square is a buzzing social spot.

Other key capitals

Every country has a quirky and fascinating capital worth exploring. Whether it be ancient temples, fairy-tale castles, weird weather, or a fun reputation for staying up all night, there's always an irresistible reason to visit. What are you waiting for? Discover somewhere new!

Oslo, Norway
Founded by the last great Viking king, Harald Hardråde, in 1050, Oslo sits on a stunning fjord and is known for easy access to forests and islands.

La Paz, Bolivia
The highest capital in the world is 11,483 feet above sea level, so visitors often gasp in the thin air. Oddly, Bolivia is one of a few countries with two capitals: La Paz and Sucre.

Ottawa, Canada
Ottawa is unusual because residents are bilingual. The city is on the divide between French- and English-speaking provinces, so residents speak both languages.

Rabat, Morocco
Rabat, which means fortified, was built as a fortress in 1146. It became the capital in 1912. It has palm trees, a beach, and a walled *medina* (old town).

Brasília, Brazil
In 1960, Brazil moved their capital from Rio de Janeiro to Brasília, a new and preplanned city. Seen from above, the design looks like an airplane.

Budapest, Hungary

Budapest is made up of two cities, Buda and Pest, on opposite sides of the turquoise Danube River. They united in 1873.

Madrid, Spain

Madrid is legendary for its nightlife; even the kids stay up late. People end the party with a sweet snack: *churros con chocolate*–doughnut fingers dunked in melted chocolate.

Athens, Greece

Athens is Europe's oldest city. The philosophy and art of the ancient Greeks gave birth to Western civilization.

Wellington, New Zealand

Wellington is the southernmost capital and the windiest city in the world! Windy Welly is on North Island and has both beaches and rainforests.

Vienna, Austria

This old-world beauty is known for grand palaces, famous composers such as Mozart, and *Sacher torte*, a popular chocolate cake invented for a prince.

Manila, Philippines

Manila is one of the most crowded cities in the world. This mega city has skyscrapers and beautiful cathedrals.

Prague, Czech Republic

Prague's cobblestone streets and huge castle look like a scene from a fairy tale. Prague became the capital of Bohemia around 800 CE and the capital of the Czech Republic in 1993.

Vimanmek Mansion
The world's largest teakwood mansion, each room in the Vimanmek is a different color and features belongings of King Rama V and other noblemen.

Democracy Monument
This monument sits in a traffic circle on the Ratchadamnoen Klang Road and was comissioned to commemorate the Siamese Revolution of 1932.

The Grand Palace
The Grand Palace has been the official residence of the kings of Siam (and then of Thailand) since 1792. It is one of the most popular tourist attractions in Thailand.

Rajadamnern Stadium
One of the two main stadiums for Muay Thai boxing in Bangkok, the Rajadamnern Stadium was built in 1941 at the request of the prime minister.

Giant Swing
This giant swing was formerly used in an old religious ceremony that was ended after several fatal accidents.

Wat Pho
One of Bangkok's oldest temples, the Temple of the Reclining Buddha is considered the highest grade of first-class royal temples. It houses a school of Thai medicine and is the birthplace of traditional Thai massage.

The city of Bangkok, Thailand, has been around since the fifteenth century. In Thai, the city's full name is *Krung Thep Mahanakhon Amon Rattanakosin Mahinthara Ayuthaya Mahadilok Phop Noppharat Ratchathani Burirom Udomratchaniwet Mahasathan Amon Piman Awatan Sathit Sakkathattiya Witsanukam Prasit*, although people who live there just call it *Krung Thep*. Bangkok is known for its historic landmarks and vibrant street life, and it is one of the world's top tourist destinations.

Chatuchak Market
This is the largest market in Thailand. Sometimes called the JJ market, it has more than 8,000 stalls, which are divided into 27 sections.

กรุงเทพมหานคร

Wat Benchamabophit
This Buddhist temple in the Dusit district is one of the city's most beautiful temples and a major tourist attraction. It is also known as the "Marble Temple."

Siam Square
This shopping and entertainment district in Bangkok connects shopping centers and other districts by a skybridge. It is also home to CentralWorld, the largest shopping center in Thailand.

Bangkok Art and Culture Center
This arts center is Bangkok's base in the international art scene. It holds cultural events in art, theater, music, film, and design in its performance spaces.

King Rama VI Monument
This 1942 statue of King Rama VI was built to commemorate the opening of Lumpini Park on land that he donated for use as a public park and exhibition area.

53

Москва

State Historical Museum
Invading Mongols, Stone Age children, crazy tsars, and more can be found in this Russian history museum, founded in 1872. The museum is housed in a redbrick palace opposite St. Basil's Cathedral.

Red Square
This enormous cobblestone space outside the Kremlin contains the extraordinary St. Basil's Cathedral. Although wars have been fought here, it's now used for parades and concerts.

Mausoleum
The famous communist revolutionary Vladimir Lenin (1870–1924) rests embalmed in the mausoleum outside the Kremlin in Red Square. He led Russia from 1917–1924.

Planetarium
Although the great race to space is over, Russia invests big in the stars. This impressive planetarium has interactive tech exhibits and a large star hall with a cosmic light show in a 82-foot-wide dome.

Kremlin
A visit to Moscow should start at the Kremlin, which means "fortress within the city." This walled enclosure is where Moscow was founded in the fourteenth century. It is the official residence of the Russian president.

Cathedral of Christ the Savior
The first version of this gold-domed Byzantine church was completed in 1883. Soon after, Russian revolutionaries took the domes and blew up the rest of the church. Reconstruction was completed in 2000.

Muzeon Park of Arts
Over 700 sculptures of Soviet idols—mostly Stalin and Lenin—rub shoulders in this green space on the bank of the Moskva River. It's a resting place for statues pulled down after communism ended.

Bolshoi Theater

The dreamy world of the Bolshoi Ballet Company comes to life in the Bolshoi Theater, which opened in 1856. It's among the oldest and largest ballet companies in the world. Tchaikovsky's *Swan Lake* premiered here in 1877.

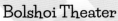

Ploshchad Revolyutsii Station

Moscow's metro stations are decorated like palaces. Stalin wanted the stations to show off communist values. Revolution Square station has colored marble as well as 76 bronze sculptures of Russian citizens.

Ivanovsky Convent

The shrine of St. John the Baptist in Moscow was built in 1604 and rebuilt in the 1860s after a fire. It was a prison for royal ladies, including pretend princesses.

Saint Basil's Cathedral

Standing tall in Red Square, St. Basil's was completed in 1561 for Ivan the Terrible. It's so eye-catching that it's become the symbol of Russia. The structure is a bizarre combination of nine onion domes painted magical, colorful patterns.

Moscow is the political, economic, and cultural center of Russia. It's a colossal capital—the largest in Europe—with 13.2 million residents. As a result of the oil boom, the former communist hub is now a playground for the wealthy, who come in droves to shop, eat, and party. Against the backdrop of massive political divides, it will always be famous for its magnificent fairy-tale sights such as St. Basil's Cathedral, with its colorful onion domes, and the Kremlin.

REYKJAVIK

Aurora Reykjavik
The northern lights are one of the world's greatest wonders. Before you get dazzled, discover what causes them. The Northern Lights Center uses both interactive exhibits and 4-D films to tackle it.

Perlan Saga Museum
Head to this museum by the Old Harbor to watch exciting moments from Icelandic history acted out by silicone models. From epic battles to volcanic eruptions, history comes to life.

Ráðhús (City Hall)
City Hall is the mayor's office and so much more. It sits at the edge of Lake Tjörnin, and it was designed to attract water birds such as the arctic tern and the greylag goose. Inside, the main draw is a 3-D map of Iceland.

National Museum
This museum shows Icelandic history from the first Viking settlement in the ninth century to independence from Denmark in 1944, when Iceland grew richer.

Whales of Iceland Museum

The shallow water of the Icelandic coast is an ideal whale feeding ground. Over 20 species of whale live there. Visitors can meet life-sized hand-painted models of all of them at this museum.

Reykjavík Art Museum

Iceland's largest art museum displays 17,000 pieces of art. The works of the country's most famous artists, including Erró, Kjarval, and Ásmundur Sveinsson, are featured.

Iceland sits where the Arctic Ocean meets the Atlantic. Its capital is close to the volcanic *Bláfjöll* (Blue Mountains). It was a long time before this humble farming and fishing town had wealth or power.

When Iceland became independent from Denmark in 1944, Reykjavík became the capital. It is the largest city in Iceland, and one third of all Icelanders live here. Since becoming the capital, Reykjavík has boomed! This small city is known for its spectacular natural beauty—mountains, oceans, hot springs, and the northern lights. It is also famous for its creative sense of fun—fun art, fun food, and fun festivals.

Harpa

This sleek concert hall on the waterfront opened in 2011. It is known for its 3-D glass panels that change color with the weather and the seasons.

Settlement Exhibition

A high-tech display surrounding tenth-century Viking artifacts makes you feel like you are walking through an ancient Viking village.

Klambratún

A well-loved spot for a game of frisbee or soccer, as well as a picnic with friends. The park is also home to the Kjarvalsstaðir Art Museum.

Hallgrímskirkja

The design of this white concrete church was inspired by the way the lava from Iceland's volcanoes cools into basalt rock. You can see this landmark from anywhere in town.

Tjörnin

The heart of old Reykjavík is Lake Tjörnin. Visitors come to view over 40 species of different birds.

BERLIN

Tiergarten
Developed in the eighteenth and nineteenth centuries, Tiergarten is an enormous 519-acre urban park, popular for everything from picnics and sports to sunbathing.

Berlin Zoo
More than 19,000 animals live at the Berlin Zoo, more than any other zoo in the world! The zoo was founded in 1844 by King Frederick William IV, who donated land and some beasts from his own menagerie.

Quite possibly the hippest capital in Europe, Berlin is an exciting city to explore. From 1961 to 1989, a huge concrete wall divided the city. When the Berlin Wall came down, the city celebrated. The capital of Germany became an urban monument to multiculturalism and freedom. Berlin has 180 museums, hosts fun events, and is famous for street art. There is interesting graffiti almost everywhere, and some of it is even part of outdoor art galleries such as the East Side Gallery.

Reichstag
Built in 1894 and rebuilt in 1999 to repair war damage, this iconic glass-dome building is the seat of the German Parliament. Visitors can take a trip to the top of the dome for stunning views.

Brandenburg Gate
This awe-inspiring neoclassical gate was modeled on the Acropolis in Athens. It's the last surviving gate of 18 in Berlin's old city wall.

Altes Museum, Museum Island

Berlin Cathedral Church
King Frederick William IV had this lavish Italian renaissance church built in 1905 for his family. Highlights include a 7,269-pipe Sauer organ and a great view from the top.

Unter den Linden
Named after the linden trees that line the way, this elegant boulevard runs through central Berlin from the Brandenburg Gate to Berlin City Palace.

Holocaust Memorial
This overwhelming and evocative memorial for the Jews murdered during the Holocaust consists of 2,711 tomb-like concrete slabs arranged in a maze near the Brandenburg Gate.

East Side Gallery
When the Berlin Wall came down in 1989, the surviving mile stretch became the world's largest open-air mural collection, with 101 powerful paintings.

Checkpoint Charlie
The most well-known border crossing from East to West Germany was Checkpoint Charlie. The museum shows the ways people sneaked out, from flying hot-air balloons to hiding in car trunks.

Berlin Wall Memorial
During the Cold War, a 87-mile concrete wall divided the city into West and East Berlin. The wall became a global symbol of oppression. The memorial tells the story of the wall, which fell in 1989.

Jewish Museum
This striking building houses the history of Jews in Germany, from the Middle Ages through to the present day.

Capitals of the World

Where in the world will you go? Pick a continent and a capital city, and get ready to embark on an adventure. The cities featured in this book are marked in bold on the map, but why stop there? There are countless others to discover, and we've included many of them on this page. Explore the sand-swept Great Pyramids near Cairo or the canal streets of Amsterdam. Peek into the mysterious Forbidden City in Beijing or the buzzing market stalls of New Delhi and Kuala Lumpur. Wander the fairy-tale castle of Prague or the wondrous galleries of the Louvre in Paris. Do you want to gaze at the snow-capped mountains surrounding La Paz in Bolivia, the highest capital city in the world? Or perhaps you would prefer to visit the futuristic skyscrapers of Astana in Kazakhstan, one of our planet's newest capital cities? There's a whole world out there for you to explore, so what are you waiting for? It's time to go!

• Nuuk

North America
There are 23 countries in North America, the biggest being Canada. The most populated city is Mexico City, with 9 million residents.

• Ottawa

• Washington, D.C.

• Havana

Mexico City •

San José •

• Caracas

• Quito

• Lima

La Paz •

• Brasília

Santiago •

• **Buenos Aires**

South America
There are 12 independent countries in South America. The largest, both in terms of land and population, is Brazil. Forty percent of South America is covered by rainforest; the largest is the Amazon, which is home to many of the world's plant and animal species.

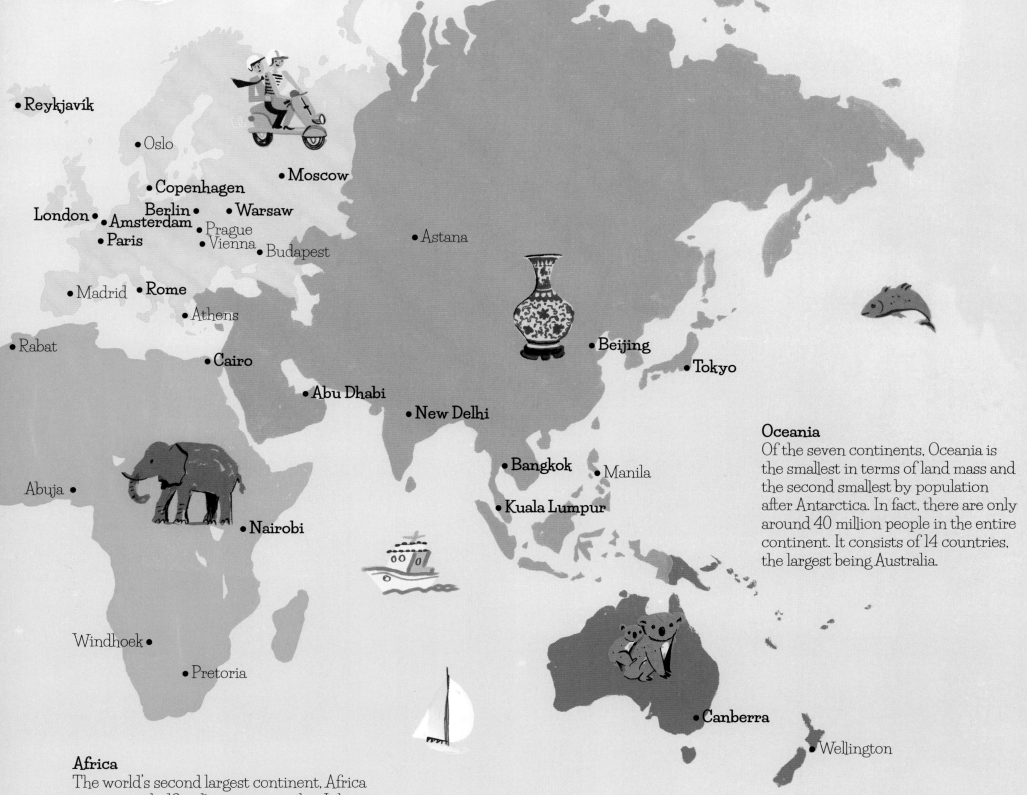

Europe

Here, you will find one of the most compact combinations of nationalities and people on the planet. Ancient Greek mariners came up with the idea of treating Europe separately from Asia, although the land connects.

Asia

This is the largest continent with the most residents. It covers one-third of Earth's surface. Sixty percent of the world's population lives here. Divided into 48 countries, three of them (Russia, Kazakhstan, and Turkey) have part of their land in Europe.

• Reykjavík

• Oslo

• Moscow

• Copenhagen

London • Berlin • Warsaw
• Amsterdam
• Paris   Prague
         • Vienna • Budapest

• Astana

• Madrid • Rome

• Athens

• Rabat

• Cairo   • Beijing

• Tokyo

• Abu Dhabi

• New Delhi

Oceania

Of the seven continents, Oceania is the smallest in terms of land mass and the second smallest by population after Antarctica. In fact, there are only around 40 million people in the entire continent. It consists of 14 countries, the largest being Australia.

Abuja •

• Bangkok   • Manila

• Kuala Lumpur

• Nairobi

Windhoek •

• Pretoria

• Canberra

• Wellington

Africa

The world's second largest continent, Africa covers nearly 12 million square miles. It has the world's longest river, the Nile, and the world's largest desert, the Sahara, which is bigger than the entire United States.

Find the capital

E very capital in the world is completely unique, with its own people, culture, history, and architecture. Can you use the clues below to figure out which capital matches each picture?

2. Six palaces and castles can be found in this city.

1. This city only became the capital city of its desert country in the 1990s.

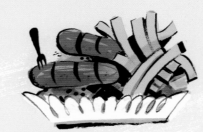

3. It is not uncommon to find people dancing in the streets of this capital.

4. The full name of this Asian capital city is a whopping 21 words long!

5. A huge concrete wall used to divide this city.

6. The only remaining Wonder of the Ancient World is found near this city.

7. The Royal Palace in this marshy capital is held up on wooden stilts.

8. This capital is home to a mysterious and ancient Forbidden City.

9. This capital city was invented because nobody could decide which city should be the capital.

10. Visiting this retro city can be like stepping back in time to the 1950s.

11. This capital city is home to some amazing Aztec ruins.

12. This city is known for its bright red buses and phone boxes.

13. This colossal capital is the largest one in Europe.

14. Home to an ancient empire, this city is full of incredible ruins.

15. The monarch of Malaysia lives in a golden-domed castle in this capital.

16. This capital is nicknamed the "City of Light."

17. This capital is known as the "World Wildlife Capital" due to its amazing native animals.

18. The shores of this city are home to 20 species of whale.

19. This ancient city has been a capital on and off since the sixth century BCE.

20. This capital is home to monuments, memorials, and the largest library in the world.

21. Known as Phoenix City, this capital has been destroyed and rebuilt more than once.

22. This city is a mixture of peaceful tradition and pop culture.

1. Abu Dhabi. 2. Copenhagen. 3. Buenos Aires. 4. Bangkok. 5. Berlin. 6. Cairo. 7. Amsterdam. 8. Beijing. 9. Canberra. 10. Havana. 11. Mexico City. 12. London. 13. Moscow. 14. Rome. 15. Kuala Lumpur. 16. Paris. 17. Nairobi. 18. Reykjavik. 19. New Delhi. 20. Washington, D.C. 21. Warsaw. 22. Tokyo.

B

Blueprint
E D I T I O N S

An imprint of Bonnier Publishing USA
251 Park Avenue South, New York, NY 10010

Author: Taraneh Ghajar Jerven
Illustrators: Nik Neves, Nina de Camargo
Editorial: Susie Rae, Lydia Halliday
Design: Shahid Mahmood

Manufactured in China

Printed in Guang Dong, China
Printer code 0080618

First Edition
2 4 6 8 10 9 7 5 3 1

Library of Congress Cataloging-in-Publication Data is available upon request.

ISBN 978-1-4998-0696-0

bonnierpublishingusa.com